Frank Truman

Mohammad Abedi

Title: Frank Truman

Author: Mohammad Abedi

Publisher: Hermes Publishing House

ISBN: 978-0-7013-0891-9

Don't look for meaning in the words. Listen to the silences.

Samuel Beckett

To the great man of world literature. An artist with deep originality and deeper purity. To dear Samuel Beckett...

Mohammad Abedi

Character in the play

Frank Truman

Act 1

The curtain rises in silence. Frank Truman is lying on the floor next to the books. The lampshade at the end of the stage is on and the ceiling lamp also shines a little light on the stage. The clock on the table rings. Frank Truman sits down. He takes a deep breath, coughs a few times. He is looking for his glasses, which are hidden among the books.

FRANK TRUMAN

{As he looks for his glasses, his hand
lands on them and the glass breaks}

I peed in this life.

He puts his glasses on his eyes, picks up his cane from the ground and walks slowly. Only the sound of his footsteps and the sound of the cane hitting the wooden floor reverberates in the hall. The sound of the cane dominates the sound of his steps.

FRANK TRUMAN

{He glances at the audience and goes
to the refrigerator on the left side of
the stage}

How disgusting it is when I feel that
everyone is watching me. Being under
surveillance is bullshit. All of you who have
come to see me now, what kind of people
are you?

{Opens the refrigerator door}

Don't you follow the news?

{He takes an apple from the
refrigerator and closes the door}

Shouldn't you look for shelter now? I am
here because I don't care a bit.

{He takes a bite of the apple}

Now this world wants to be destroyed
tomorrow or 5 centuries later, it wants to
be destroyed with an atomic bomb or with
any other shit.

{He nonchalantly puts the apple in his mouth and pauses for a few seconds. He bites the apple and then picks up a newspaper from the floor and goes to one of the audiences with his cane. He gently taps the shoulder of the audience with a cane, and takes the newspaper towards the audience}

Are you educated? Take it and read it.

{He hands the newspaper to the audience and returns to the stage}

He throws the rest of the apple on the ground and pushes it a little ahead of his feet with his cane.

FRANK TRUMAN

Do you know what an ultimatum is?

{He picks up the dictionary from the floor and turns the pages. He walks slowly and reads in a teacher-like tone}

Ultimatum, in diplomacy, is a final written warning from a government to another government about doing something or fulfilling a demand that is not being paid attention to.

{He pauses for a few moments}

It may lead to war or hostile actions. Hostile actions!

{He laughs}

I am sure that tomorrow morning, nothing will be left of all of us except a handful of ashes, neither I matter, nor you, nor my words, nor your words. we are going to die

{He pauses}

Well, to hell! These atomic bombs were made from scratch so that we would die. If I had looked at the world like a rooster from the very beginning, I wouldn't have been sad at all. I have never seen a rooster get so upset that he smokes or scrapes a vein in his hand with a razor in the bathroom.

Frank sits on the chair behind the table, takes a cigarette from his cigarette pack and lights it with a match, takes a large bag, takes out the radio inside the bag. Takes out a large number of tapes from the desk drawer and places them on the table (these tapes are arranged by year). He picks up one of the tapes after checking it, reads it, and blows it with his mouth. The dirt on the tape flies. He opens the tape compartment of the radio and puts the tape inside. He is silent and smokes.

FRANK TRUMAN {Tape}

August 8, 1945, Hiroshima, Japan.

Even though the nurse looks a lot like Snow White and her voice is like an angel, I just asked her to bring something to record my voice. After a few days, they pulled me out from under the rubble of the ruined houses. Where are the tapes I recorded? They must be destroyed. Ah! I wish only my father would be destroyed. I don't know if I am lucky or unlucky; But anyway, I survived. I survived, what will happen? The country is destroyed. To hell though. It is not my country. I was studying here and it's all the fault of that stupid father. Former father! Now he is dead and I am left and the money that will come to me from the sale of the house after his death. Of course, I don't think there is anything left from our house that I can sell after this black rain. I didn't want to study in Japan. My father, now that the atomic bomb must have turned him into a handful of alcohol-tainted ash, tried hard to become a part of the Hiroshima Brewing Company, so that he could remain an alcoholic and come home with a glass of beer every night, and work. His efforts paid off and he was hired; But a month later, the company's board of directors realized that my father is a better customer than an employee. They fired him very quickly. Even beer companies wouldn't hire a blind drunk like my dad. After he was fired, he stayed in Japan and did everything, and naturally I had to stay. My mother died when I was seven years old, in 1934, and I was left alone to endure my father's morals and his stupid decisions in drunkenness. We didn't have financial problems, but everything was in a mess. I always hated my father, but he tried very hard so that I could study safely and get accepted to Tokyo University. Now that I'm left alone, I don't think I want to study or stay in Japan at all. The nurse told me how lucky I am. She told me that they are going to transfer me from this gray Hiroshima to a better hospital in Nagasaki very quickly. I am much better than others. Because they are dead! I only have a lot of pain in my chest, my left leg is tied from the knee down, the fingers of my right hand and my left wrist are bandaged. On my forehead, as if an expressionist painter painted a big red wound. On my forehead, as if an expressionist painter painted a big red wound. it is nothing. I'm going to Nagasaki from this wreck. Happy ten years since I came to Japan. I will be eighteen in a few months. I peed in this life. I'm tired.

Frank presses a button and takes the tape out of the radio. He goes to the refrigerator. His foot slips on the remaining apple and falls on the ground. He stays on the ground for several seconds and then gets up and throws the rest of the apple towards the audience. He goes back to the refrigerator and takes an apple and takes a few bites, then puts it in his mouth. He has an apple in his mouth and is staring at the audience. He bites the apple. His tooth is like a pair of scissors and the rest of the apple is like a human whose hanging rope has been torn and he falls to the ground in this state. He walks a little and stands facing the audience.

FRANK TRUMAN

{With a funny laugh}

The same day that I arrived, the United States dropped an atomic bomb on Nagasaki

{laughs again}

Sometimes I feel that I was the cause of all the nonsense events in history. I am the cursed man of history. Maybe it's not bad that I die; But apparently, I am doomed to be immortal. An immortal 97-year-old man. I had to stay in Japan for a while, I continued to live a little and I couldn't bear it. I went to China from Japan. Was it because I was cursed or what, but everyone had hammers and sickles in their hands, with blood dripping from them on their flags, and they wanted to lead their lives to shine with those two tools. Wherever I was, it was somehow pulled into a wedge. Exactly when I went to Korea, the Korean

War started, every important coup that happened in the world, it was as if an invitation had been sent to me in advance to witness it closely. When I went anywhere in this muddy globe, a misfortune happened. This case has two cases:

1) There is a God who wants to tell me that I love you so much, that wherever I want this world to be destroyed, I will protect you. Even if everyone is poor and destroyed.

2) Maybe there is a God who wants to tell me that I am so sick of you, that wherever you go in the world, I want all the people in that part of the world to be destroyed, and I will not let you die until you understand how much I hate you.

{Pauses for a few moments}

Of course, maybe there is another case:

There is a God for whom my existence is not as important as a piece of wedge. And he doesn't care where I am and what I'm doing. If the third situation is correct, I have to say

{Raises his voice}

You are not as important to me as a piece of wedge too.

{He shows the middle finger of his left hand towards the sky. He is holding the cane with his right hand}

He sits at the table and lights a new cigarette. Frank goes through the tapes and finds one. He puts it on the radio.

FRANK TRUMAN (tape)

December 1959, Paris, France

Is life more absurd than making a snowman? You fight for a long time to finally enjoy something whose destruction is certain. What a stupid circus! People care about others as much as they care about their own snowman. They leave what they built so easily to burn and melt. To be destroyed. Do I have the right to complain about the one who made and shaped me and left me? I was crushed snow under the feet of selfish people who consider the earth to be their father's inheritance. She picked up my pieces from the cold fields of Leningrad. At that time, nothing kept me alive except writing. It was as if I always had to run away like a criminal so that no one knew anything about me and the most interesting thing is that no one wanted to know anything about me. I lost all my money in gambling to an old Chinese man named Shi Han and took refuge in Russia.

At the same moment when the mental pressure caused by working too much in the production line of a cake and cookies factory was bothering me, at the same time when life was so boring for me that even the smell of Leningradsky cake made me feel nauseous, and even smoking Belomorkanal after finishing the work did not make me feel good at all, I saw her. I had accepted for a long time that I am an ordinary person and that my life is not going to have light. Human beings gradually realize that he is nothing. It's hard at first, but then you get used to it.

Nobody is nothing. It doesn't make much of a difference. In a really funny way, if you look closely, Einstein and I are not much different. Now I am a bit more handsome than him and my voice is better, he is also a bit more intelligent; But both of us are generally the same. In fact, both of us are nothing. He has fought more to prove to himself that this is not the case. I fought less.

I was burying all my imaginations of a beautiful world next to the cakes, snow, blizzard, cigarettes, coupons and food baskets. Not that everything is pure dirt, but I didn't want life like this. This was different from what I imagined. In my imagination, I was never supposed to lose and be so miserable at the age of thirty-three that my only reason to be alive is that my heart hasn't failed yet. One night, I, who had seen since childhood how hateful my father was when he was drunk, drank so much vodka with one of my friends in a cafe bar on Nevsky Street that I could not speak. I saw her. She worked in that cafe.

She was like a sun and I stared at her and was amazed. A little later, I realized that everyone was looking at her. She was mesmerizing. Every day after work I went to that cafe to see her. She also knew this and I thought that her feelings for me were mutual.

My life was empty of all those ideals of my youth, this time I enjoyed my inner animal more than anything else. In the end, it was instinct that ruled. I had tried all my life to be successful in my work and to become a great person so that when I come to the truth of my existence, which is instinct, no one criticizes me. I had fallen in love with her.

After a while, she stopped working in the café. She left this job, but she also comes to the cafe. Sometimes she sits next to me, sometimes somewhere else. All the men who were in that cafe invited her to their table. Me, I think no one really liked her. This was the first time that my whole world became one person, and I changed my life just to attract her attention. A little later, without her telling me, I realized from her behavior that she has the same behavior with everyone. She started dancing with one of the people who came to this cafe every night, and I was so tormented to see her, who did not take care of herself; But now that I'm away from her, I have to tell myself that I wasn't taking care of myself more. I was careless about myself. When I saw a series of these behaviors, I left there without showing my broken heart to her.

Sometimes I think that she loved me too. I will never understand this. This is the nature of the world. You never know who is thinking of you in private. Just as no one knows exactly what you are thinking in private. I am now the same snowman who dreams that the sun will come. Even if it kills him. I came to de Gaulle's France to...

Frank turns off the radio and removes the tape. While holding a cane, he goes to the refrigerator. He opens the refrigerator door and takes an apple and does not close the refrigerator door. He looks at it for a few seconds with deep breaths. He spits on the ground. The constant beeping of the refrigerator breaks the silence of the scene. Frank is in the same position for several seconds and then slams the refrigerator door hard. He takes a knife and a plate from the top of the refrigerator. He puts the apple in the plate and goes to the chair. He sits on it, puts one leg over the other and looks at the audience as he peels the apple with a knife.

FRANK TRUMAN

At that time, Charles de Gaulle wanted to do everything to make France strong again. He did this. He was always talking about glory. From the independence of Europe and its freedom. The independence and freedom that he wanted to bring to France with nuclear weapons. All of them really achieved some of their goals, and in this way, they destroyed many people. If I don't want to see the glory of a country, what should I do? Politicians are all scoundrels and most of the people only play the role of good people. Every fool knew at the same time that these nuclear weapons may appear to be a deterrent to war, but one day they will be used again. Tomorrow...

{Frank gets up}

Your presence here is so ridiculous that I don't know what tone to choose to talk to you. Next to me, what are you looking for that is more important than your death? Tomorrow the atomic bomb will destroy all of you and what do you want to say to yourself? Do you want to tell yourself that in the last moments of your life, you sat down and listened to the nonsense of a hundred-year-old old man? Don't you have any love? Nothing to write, nothing to do before you die? Of course, this is also understandable. When you know that you will definitely die tomorrow, and there is no other person alive, you act as absurdly as you are going to die. Instead of walking with your love, instead of going to a place you always wanted to go there but you didn't have the chance, because you thought there was too much opportunity, it's not strange to come and sit and listen to the radio of someone like me whose life is not better than you, not worse. I was like you.

If I want to be honest with you, I am happy that you are here because there is no one to listen to me; But I also sympathize with you.

{goes to a female audience}

Excuse me, lady! Do you have anyone you want to talk to before you die? All the people I wanted to talk to died. Are all the people you like to talk to dead?

{Frank Truman will wait for the answer and will have improvised reactions according to it and continue the text after the reactions}

You know what? You know you will die tomorrow, and tomorrow all those people will die too. Do you like to keep your unsaid words, when they will turn into nothing in less than two days, and bury them, or at least say them before you die? Of course, why do you want to say it? What will happen? one has understood yet. Why should you talk to someone now? Those unsaid words that you reviewed with yourself in your privacy and never told anyone, have shaped you and maybe you are afraid that by saying them and not getting the reaction you want, will destroy your formed character, which is like a solid wall or a fragile wall, with a smile. Your wall will probably collapse; But my daughter! Please know this. Your wall will fall anyway. It is your choice how you want to fall. Personally, I always put the knife to my pride's throat, but when I tried to cut its throat, the knife acted like a toy. Sometimes I wanted to kill my pride, but I never could. This made me often not achieve many things that I can say in my privacy how much self-esteem I had and I was able to overcome many things. Maybe it was because of the wrong people who came into my life. As soon as they see that I took the knife to sacrifice my identity for them, like a chameleon, they change their color and forget everything.

This is a human trait my daughter! Anything more unattainable is more attractive. The same unattainable thing, if you reach it, it will be worthless to you than a piece of garbage.

That's what vapidness means. Not everyone is like this; But that's what most people are. They have no capacity and are forgetful. I was even like that myself sometimes.

When a wall collapses, it cannot be rebuilt. Even if it is rebuilt, that wall is no longer the same wall as before.

Frank picks up a book from the floor, goes back to the table and lights a cigarette. Inserts a new tape into the radio.

FRANK TRUMAN (tape)

November 9, 1989, Berlin

{with a stressed and crazy tone}

It collapsed. Great damn wall of Berlin! I think it's been a month since I was admitted to this mental hospital for attempting suicide. If these bitches had arrived just an hour later, I wouldn't be alive now; But now I am still breathing. I know that I will die soon and cancer will put me to sleep in the cradle of death like a loving mother. Suicide for me was only hastening my death. I know that I will die very soon; But I wanted it to be sooner than usual. It is not the pain that bothers me. The fact that after more than 60 years of life, there is no one to ask how I am, makes me understand how stupid I was. Maybe I was really a bad person that no one even asks about my death. Maybe in my illusion, I was an interesting and good person.

Illusion is intoxicating, like the gas I opened at home and it was killing me, and I am intoxicated by the poisonous gas that the books I read breathed into my lungs. The same books that wanted to help me be a better person and make a better world. I couldn't make a better world. I didn't become a better person myself. There are so many people who have not even touched the books that kill their souls and they are not alone. Human gets meaning in relation to others. Some people instinctively choose loneliness. They were chosen to choose loneliness. When someone is lonely and involuntarily chooses loneliness, loneliness becomes an impenetrable wall for him. Not a glass wall like the Berlin Wall! Every wall will collapse one day. Except this damn wall!

Loneliness is the mother of all miseries and if this shit did not exist, I could bear the rest of the pain. A person can reduce his pains with others, but in solitude, even the smallest pains intensify in an exaggerated way. Did I say anything about the Berlin Wall? Han? Because I don't care. Because all this is ridiculous. So what? What is the wall? What is the door? What is the country? Where is the east, where is the west? We are getting sick! We are getting sick!

> {he shouts louder and the sound of the nurses' footsteps is heard, who are trying to control him}

Let me go

> {he shouts}

Let me go, you bastards

> {shouting}

At least let me stop the recording, you bastard.

Frank cries and slams the book down hard. He goes from one side of the stage to the other side of the stage with a cane like guards. He goes to the refrigerator. He takes an apple and goes to the audience.

FRANK TRUMAN

I always wanted to be able to face the politicians of the world one day, and tell them, do you think I'm stupid? It is true that I am not strong enough for you, but don't think that I am stupid. When I remember my past, I want to die. I could have died many times and I did not. Maybe I needed a grand finale. So that one day some people will know me and listen to me. I'm Frank Truman {shakes one of the audiences' hands}. Apparently, a person! that now, apart from one time of my life which I think ended too soon, I am experiencing my happiest moment. Beside you.

Because I know that we are all going to die tomorrow, I know that you are not going to hurt me after hearing what I said. I like you

{he hugs the person who gave him the newspaper at the beginning of the show. Then he gives the apple to a different audience}

Put it in your mouth!

{turns away from the audience}

In the same years in France, I married a German lady. Irma Muller. Later, Billy Wilder also made a movie with the same name; Irma la Douce. But my Irma was really more beautiful than her Irma. Her eyes carried the sadness of the defeat of two world wars and her voice was hotter than a crematorium. At her request, we went to Germany after marriage and according to my eternal curse, which I talked about with you, shortly after, they built the Berlin Wall.

We were in Weissensee, located in East Berlin. A small area in Pankow, Germany. My Irma was a dress designer and I worked as a translator. From the dream of writing my own novels and texts, I had come to translate other people's nonsense.

{with a happy tone}

But it didn't matter at all. I had Irma. Irma was a 162 cm band-aid that cured all my pains from childhood until that moment.

I am about 100 years old. 97. The first thirty-three years of my life were a wedge. The second thirty-three years of my life, next to Irma, were great; and the third thirty-three years of my life is the garbage you see. My life changes every thirty years. Damn these politicians! I am coming to the end of my third thirty-three years of life and I am going to be happy again, but they are going to drop an atomic bomb. Wedge to their graves.

I had the honor of living with Irma for 28 years, and it was as if she was born to soothe a suffering person like me. I myself was full of suffering, but it was me who turned from a worthless stone into a diamond. It was a beautiful and valuable painting of pain and suffering, but I got meaning from her. I came to believe that life can be beautiful even with one person. But life is like a crazy writer who if he feels that you can guess him, he will change everything for you at any cost so that you understand that you will not repeat this mistake again.

I thought I was only going to experience happiness. On the first day of 1987, we went to Friedrichshain to have some fun and one day, when I was smoking a cigarette on the Oberbaum bridge, next to the beautiful Irma, and watching her beauty, on the other side, we saw a girl and a boy kissing each other and crying. They held each other's hands. We also held each other's hands. We understood them deeply.

Suddenly the boy jumped down from the bridge. The girl started screaming and we quickly ran towards her so that at least she wouldn't make this mistake. The East German People's Police quickly came towards us. The girl ran to the police and it was clear that if they fought on equal terms, with her anger and sadness, she could kill ten policemen. But the bullet of the People's Police changed the game. I cursed him loudly and felt the butt of the gun on my head and I fell.

In total blackness, I heard the roar of a woman and then, the sound of another bullet. I wish no bullet would ever extinguish my Irma's sea eyes forever. I wish the butt of the gun would hit Irma's head and I would get shot.

{in a very gentle voice}

No! No! I wish I had both. Damn Oberbaum bridge. This bridge is called the bridge of the death of my life. The bridge that destroyed my world. The bridge that took my Irma from me. Sometimes I think that the gun butt hit caused my cancer, but I remember that my cancer was lung cancer and the main cause was a lot of cigarettes that I smoked before Irma's death, because of the happiness of being with her, and after Irma's death, because of the sadness of her absence. Damn smoking!

Frank sits on a chair. A few seconds of absolute silence. He gets up.

FRANK TRUMAN

Damn smoking!

He puts a cigarette on his lips, lights it and wants to record a new tape. He looks at the audience.

FRANK TRUMAN

I wish I could play all the tapes for you; But you don't want to, nor do I enjoy remembering myself. Don't you want to leave here?

{laughs loudly}

Puts the new tape in the radio.

FRANK TRUMAN (tape)

Westeros, Sweden, unknown date

I don't know how many years I haven't left the house. Two things in my life are immortal. journey, and suffering; But I still don't understand whether it is this journey that creates pain or this pain that makes me pack my bag every time to travel. Uppsala University invited me to give me an honorary doctorate. In the years after Irma's death and my cancer death, I taught poor children in different countries and translated many novels. Work was an opiate that made me forget many things more easily. Not to forget, but to ease my suffering. Work was opium and living life was a big sandpaper that was drawn on the saddest part of my life's memories and reduced its sadness. Now, I accept even my sadness with love. Because there is nothing for me but myself. Like a child that is born, and maybe a little ugly {bitter, laughs}. But you are a father. You accept everything because it is your product. Sadness, suffering, happiness, anger and thousands of other nonsense feelings, these are all my products. The product of my choice, the product of the work I did, or even the product of the work I did not do. Sometimes luck and other things.

Now I am going to be honored for my teaching in Mandia in India, Lampung in Indonesia, Ghazghan in Uzbekistan and several other cities from other countries, and I don't want to get up from my bed.

From one age onwards, if you are very interested in life, as soon as you wake up, it is a great blessing for you; But what if you are not interested? I am not very interested in life; But I am very afraid. I am afraid of becoming nothing. I prefer being in pain to not existing. From a certain age, thinking about how your life went, and reviewing your memories, becomes more attractive to you than your life itself. Like a football player, who after retirement, reviews the video of his football games. This may be a kind of projection. A kind of escape from remembering that you are old and more vulnerable than ever. An escape that makes you forget that you are not very efficient anymore. All your acquaintances, all the people whose memories you are reviewing, have died or are dying.

Every morning I drink coffee with the angel of death, have lunch with her, listen to music with her, sleep with her, even talk with her.

The smallest pain in my body makes me think I'm going to die now. I am drowning more than ever in the sea of fantasies, and my thoughts and fantasies about what I did and didn't do are flesh-eating fish that sometimes bite me with all their strength.

Mr. Thunberg's daughter is like a rope that pulls me out of the sea of fantasies every day at 12 noon and saves me from drowning. By knocking on the door a few times and bringing a good meal. Every time, a problem conquers a person's whole being and mind, and he thinks that he has never experienced such mental hardship before; But it's a lie. It has always been the same. When you accept this, your life will be worse than ever.

Aging and loneliness together, is like eating the rat poison and cyanide together, and there is no escape from either of them. Loneliness makes a person old, and old age makes a person lonely.

I may not go to Uppsala University. An honorary doctorate is not really important to me at this age. A person sometimes tries to attract the attention of others. My others all died. I don't care about anyone's opinion. No one!

Frank sits on the sofa. Silence fills the space and the only thing that can be heard is the sound of his cane slowly tapping the ground

{this tapping of the cane has a precise time order (every 4 seconds)}

He lights a cigarette and goes to the audience.

FRANK TRUMAN

{To one of the audiences}

If you are like me, kill yourself before you get old. Although you are not old now. You will definitely die tomorrow, so don't worry about anything.

> {He moves his hand and says in a very, very insignificant tone}

Stay alive!

Frank returns to the stage and sits on a chair. Silence covers the scene. He goes to the radio, puts in a tape and hits the record button.

FRANK TRUMAN

Hello!

He stops recording. He hits the play button and listens to his "Hello" voice. After making sure that his radio and recorder are still working, he looks at the audience in silence for several seconds. He hits the record button, lights a cigarette.

FRANK TRUMAN

> {recording}

> {announces the date of the same day as the show}

Location unknown

This is the most absurd thing I am doing

{a little silence}

My most absurd tape, my last tape. A bunch of people are sitting in front of me and I don't know why they are there

{very funny and helpless tone}

Tomorrow they will drop an atomic bomb on us and this tape is being recorded so that it will be destroyed with us, but I am recording it. My last tape is the same as life. I am living even though my destruction is certain.

I am recording this tape even though no trace of it is supposed to remain. What kind of dirt are we? We are toys, for those who are toys. We are captives of captives and prisoners of prisoners. Matches for matches. My absence is your absence, and I'm not supposed to be, so you won't be either. It started with the atom and ended with the atomic bomb.

{Laughs}

I don't care! I wish they would drop an atomic bomb at least tomorrow at noon, so that I can have a cup of coffee and smoke a cigarette in the morning.

I want to know which person is going to press the button to fire the bomb, and I really wish from the bottom of my heart that he doesn't die and lives at least as long as me, and talks with that beautiful finger when he is alone

{looks at his index finger}.

I'm tired of always being anxious like a fool about your fake power play and sad, destructive pride. My Irma was killed by your ridiculous games, my father was killed by your games, so is my soul. I prefer you to kill me sooner than to rape me every day, you bastards! I am tired of your games. Finish it as soon as possible.

{Silence for three seconds}

Good night!

Frank Truman takes a deep breath and stops the recording, slowly gets up, lies on the floor and sleeps. After 7 seconds of silence, the stage goes dark.

www.ingramcontent.com/pod-product-compliance
Lightning Source LLC
Chambersburg PA
CBHW020444030426
42337CB00014B/1391